S0-DZC-309

My Baby Sister

Written by Meg Stein

Photography by Michael Curtain

sundance **Newbridge**

Purchased With
Title I Funds

This is my baby sister.

My baby sister can read.

She can read with me.

My baby sister can play.

She can play with me.

My baby sister can eat.

She can eat with me.

My baby sister can smile.

She can smile with me.

My baby sister can sleep.